Especially for

_____

With love from

_____

To Ellison, Luke, Kaitlyn, Hunter, Mallory, Rhett,
Eileen, Deivis, Leah, and the rest of our awesome
Sunday school class—the reign starts now!
—Jordan

For my awesome art helpers, Kate and Ellison.
—Jonathan

All Scripture quotations are taken from the Holy Bible, New
International Version®, NIV®. Copyright © 1973, 1978, 1984, 2011
by Biblica Inc.™ Used by permission of Zondervan. All rights
reserved worldwide. (www.zondervan.com). The "NIV" and
"New International Version" are trademarks registered in the
United States Patent and Trademark Office by Biblica Inc.™

Copyright © 2024 by Jordan Raynor

All rights reserved.

Published in the United States by WaterBrook, an imprint of
Random House, a division of Penguin Random House LLC.

WATERBROOK and colophon are registered trademarks of
Penguin Random House LLC.

ISBN 978-0-593-19315-0
Ebook ISBN 978-0-593-19316-7

The Library of Congress catalog record is available at
https://lccn.loc.gov/2022042530.

Printed in China

waterbrookmultnomah.com

10 9 8 7 6 5 4 3 2 1

First Edition

Cover art and interior illustrations by Jonathan D. Voss

Book and cover design by Sonia Persad using a design
established by Patrice Sheridan

Most WaterBrook books are available at special quantity
discounts for bulk purchase for premiums, fundraising,
and corporate and educational needs by organizations,
churches, and businesses. Special books or book excerpts
also can be created to fit specific needs. For details, contact
specialmarketscms@penguinrandomhouse.com.

The Royal in You

written by **Jordan Raynor**

WATERBROOK

illustrated by **Jonathan D. Voss**

ON A DAY COMING SOON,
though nobody knows when . . .

We'll look up at the sky and see heaven descend.

Jesus said He won't stay in the clouds way up there.

He'll bring heaven to earth, and He'll live with us here.

When heaven comes down,
we'll all rush to meet Jesus,
bringing paintings, inventions,
and gifts for Him with us.

When we long at last reach our final destination,

we'll hug long-lost loved ones from every nation.

Then we'll all turn and stare at God's epic new world
and the city He made out of gold, gems, and pearls.

As we step through the gates, we will all be in awe

that a city can stand seven million feet tall.

There will be no more sin, no more sickness or sadness,

just the best things made perfect, bringing God and us gladness.

The sun will stay set, and the moon will be gone,

as God's radiant light blurs the dusk into dawn.

But the best part by far is
King Jesus will be there,
making everything new with
His peace, love, and care.

And now you might think that our story is ending,

but in fact, this is just the beginning.

Because Jesus wants you to *rule* with Him—

to explore and fill the kingdom of heaven with Him.

For kingdoms have more than just people and kings.

They have art and bakeries, campfires and swings.

God says He won't rule this world all on His own—

He'll send princes and princesses out from His throne.

To ride without fear on the backs of great lions

and blaze brand-new trails through the middle of Zion.

And to master the flute, piano, or timpani
as Jesus applauds your brilliant symphony.

Perhaps you will bulldoze roads for new cities

or help lead the Jesus welcome committee.

Or create a new sport with no need to worry about getting hurt or needing to hurry.

You might spend time learning new subjects and skills,
with no fear of testing or loud fire drills.

Maybe you'll explore galaxies far, far away

and marvel at what God once made in a day.

So don't think for one second that heaven is boring,

because we'll be reigning, creating, and exploring!

Not just for our joy, and surely not for our glory,

but to love and to worship the One who is worthy.

It'll be so much better than your wildest dreams—

ruling heaven on earth next to Jesus our King.

Note to Parents

I would have never admitted this to my parents or pastor, but when I was growing up, I *dreaded* the thought of heaven. From what I could tell, heaven was a place in the clouds without the things I loved most as a kid:

- no animals or pets
- no trees to climb
- no sports to play
- no paintings to paint
- nothing to do but sing and play harps forever and ever

The promise of heaven didn't fill me with hope and excitement. It filled me with fear and boredom.

It wasn't until I was an adult that I finally discovered what God's Word *actually* says about heaven. Contrary to the picture culture paints, Scripture tells us:

- Heaven won't stay in the clouds way up there. Jesus will bring heaven to earth, and He'll live with us here (see REVELATION 21:1–5).

- Heaven includes the work of God's hands—a city that stands more than seven million feet tall (see REVELATION 21:15–21)—and some of the work of *our* hands as well (see ISAIAH 60; REVELATION 21:26).

- We won't play harps for eternity. We "will reign for ever and ever" with Christ by filling, subduing, and exploring the New Earth where every human will "long enjoy" the thrilling "work of their hands" (see ISAIAH 65:17–22; REVELATION 22:5).

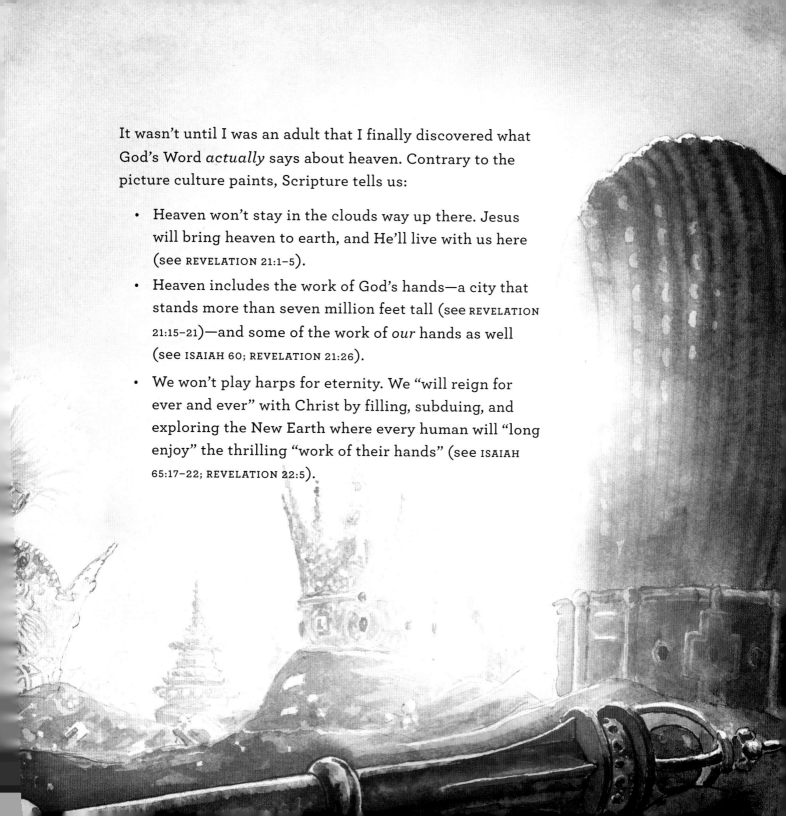

In *The Royal in You,* Jonathan and I have tried to communicate these truths in a concise and inspiring way. Our hope is that whatever negative feelings your child experienced when they thought of heaven before this book—confusion, boredom, and maybe even fear—have been replaced with clarity, excitement, and hope.

To help your kids go a level deeper into what God's Word says about heaven, I want to offer them a free gift: a devotional you can read with your kids that explores the scriptures this book is based on *and* what kids can do today to respond to the future hope of heaven.

I've also got a free gift for *you,* parent: a short ebook called *Half-Truths About Heaven.* If some of the truths in this book are as new to you as they were to me just a few years ago, this ebook will be an *immense* blessing to you.

You can access both of these free resources right now at www.jordanraynor.com/kids.

Jordan Raynor